माझ्या डोक्यावर छप्पर असण्याचा सुरक्षा करून व्यप्याचा
आणि चांगले जीवन जगण्याचा अधिकार मला आहे.

...alo Urpamb.

..., o di essere sottoposto ad essa. 나는 인종차별로부터 보호 받을 권리가 있다.

TENGO DERECHO A QUE ME PROTEJAN DEL RACISMO.

..OIT DE NE PAS ÊTRE REJETÉ À CAUSE DE MA RELIGION

..人 包圍,

من حقي ان تكون لي حماية من العنف

I have the right to be protected from violence

..ZU WERDEN. मला शाळेत जाण्याच्या अधिकार आहे.

..وریکیورارب من حقی Ik heb het recht om mezelf te uiten

..lf phymulpf nltlumm, לכאת סברות לאנגף הביה סבר בכל

..eito de riz. 遊ぶ権利 ICH HABE DAS RECHT, MICH ZU ÄUßERN.

..FFERENTLY BECAUSE I AM A GIRL. मुझे सूचित किए जाने का, खुद को व्यक्त
करने का और भाग लेने का अधिकार है

..npalo боти услышанном.

..զրգայացության րնելու: Ձս ռեalս hpmulf

..n123 sk5 upraus phtiju: J'ai le droit d'aller à l'école

..R RECHAZADO POR MI DISCAPACIDAD. 我也有被愛的權利.

ICH HABE A RECHT ZU SPIELEN.
    DAS   Ho il diritto di giocare.

..IRE

من حق دارم مورد عشق ومحبت قرار بگیرم.

나는 학교에 갈 권리가 있다.

..ובכות לא נאסר ורקים הקיהים.

من حقي ان أذهب إلى المدرسة

I HAVE THE RIGHT

REZA DALVAND

scribble

I have the right to a name
and a nationality.

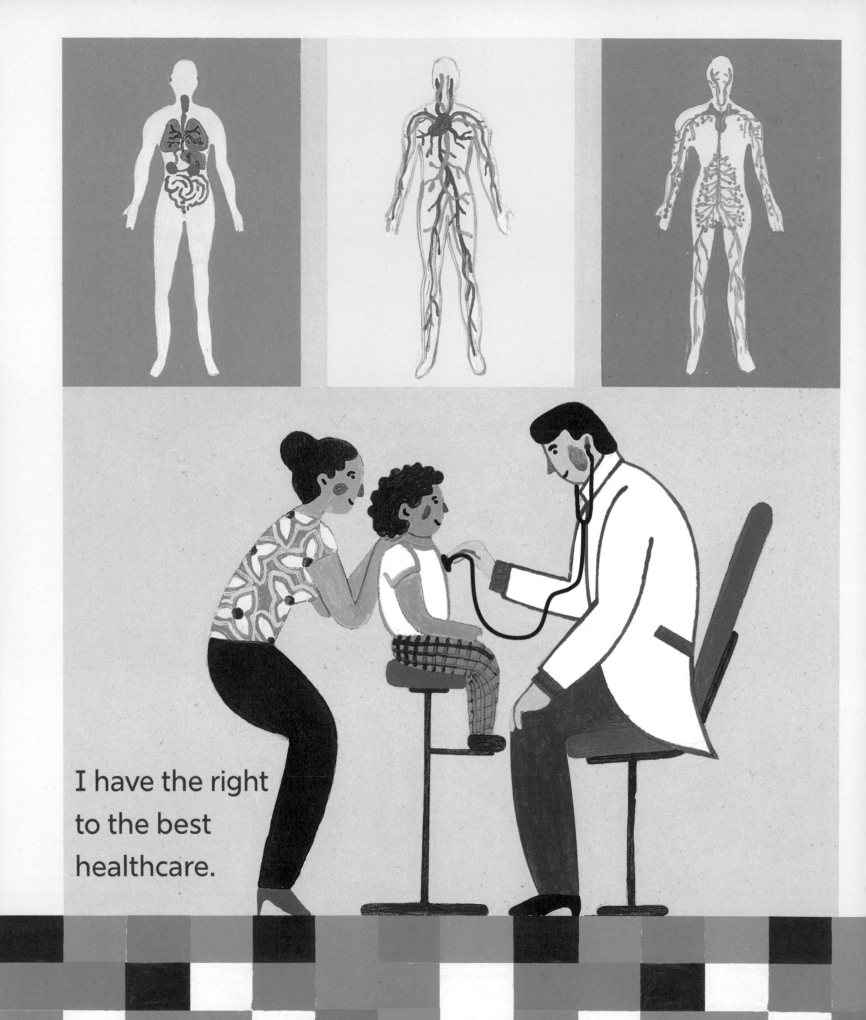

I have the right
to the best
healthcare.

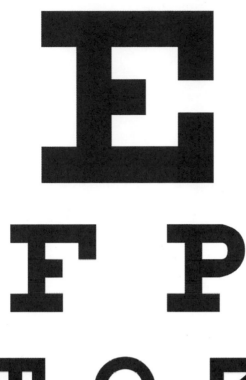

I have the right to nutritious foods.

I have the right to an education.

I have the right to a home where I can thrive.

I have the right to safety and shelter.

I have the right to be protected from violence.

I have the right to not be discriminated against for my race or nationality...

...or my gender...

…or my disability…

...or my beliefs
and those
of my family.

I have the right
to not be forced
to fight wars.

I have the right
to rest and play.

I have the right to grow up with
my family and my community.

I have the right to be loved.

In 1989, the United Nations unanimously adopted the Convention on the Rights of the Child. Today, 140 nations have signed this treaty, which commits them to defend and guarantee the rights of all children without distinction and to answer for these commitments before the United Nations. This means that in principle a child who lives in a country where these rights are applied will feel respected and considered. They will be able to grow and develop in complete safety, both emotionally and physically.

These fundamental rights are still not respected in a very large number of countries. Much progress, therefore, remains to be made for adults to realise that children must be a priority. Their development is crucial for the future of the world.

In this magnificent book, Reza Dalvand puts all his artistic talent at the service of children and their universal rights. His joyful, poetic, and lively illustrations praise their fundamental rights. In this book, it is the child themself who speaks about their rights: they speak up in a simple and direct way. It is the child who makes this fundamental subject accessible and obvious.

Reading this text is essential so that all adults never forget that all children have rights, and that children themselves know them, from an early age.

—Dr Catherine Gueguen

I am happy creating my books. Every day I find this desire to make children happy. There is nothing more beautiful. This book is particularly important to me because it carries the voice of children and makes their rights known. It is a tribute to all the children of the world, without distinction of language, ethnicity, or religion.

—Reza Dalvand

Reza Dalvand is a multi-award-winning author and illustrator from Iran. He has published more than twenty books, translated all over the world. His previous title, *Entre toi et moi*, written by Catherine Gueguen, was published by Les Arènes in 2020.

The illustrations in this book were made with oil paints,
crayons, and markers then digitally assembled.

Typeset in Rig Sans by the publisher.

Scribble, an imprint of Scribe Publications
Wurundjeri Country, 18–20 Edward Street, Brunswick, Victoria 3056, Australia
2 John Street, Clerkenwell, London, WC1N 2ES, United Kingdom
3754 Pleasant Ave, Suite 100, Minneapolis, Minnesota 55409, USA

Originally published in French as *J'ai Le Droit* by Les Arènes in 2022
This edition publicaed by Scribble in 2023

Text and illustrations © Reza Dalvand, 2022
Afterword © Catherine Gueguen, 2022
English translation © Scribble, 2023

Publisher: Miriam Rosenbloom
Editor: Bella Li
Production: Mick Pilkington

FSC
www.fsc.org
MIX
Paper from
responsible sources
FSC® C144853

This book is printed with vegetable-soy based inks, on FSC® certified paper and
other controlled materials from responsibly managed forests and other sources,
ensuring that the supply chain from forest to end-user is chain of custody certified.

Printed and bound in China by RR Donnelley.

978 1 761380 08 2 (Australian edition)
978 1 915590 08 4 (UK edition)
978 1 915590 36 7 (UK paperback edition)
978 1 957363 44 8 (US edition)

Catalogue records for this title are available from the
National Library of Australia and the British Library.

scribblekidsbooks.com
scribblekidsbooks

Scribble acknowledges the Wurundjeri Woi Wurrung of the
Kulin Nations — the first and continuing custodians of the land on
which our books are created. Sovereignty has never been ceded.
We pay our respects to Elders past and present.

나는 전쟁에 참여하지 않을 권리가 있다. Il ullero

मुझे देखभाल करने का, बीमारी से
सुरक्षित रहने का और अच्छी तरह से
पोषित होने का अधिकार है।

Ho il diritto di non andare in

Tenho o direito de ter un t

من حق دارم به مدرسه بروم. 笑う 権利 J'AI LE

Il ullero право ullers Ceúlero.

I HAVE THE RIGHT TO GO TO SCHOOL. 祝

ICH HABE DAS RECHT, NICHT WEGEN MEINER BEHINDERUNG ABGELE

Il ullero право на крошу над головой. شَ باشم.

HO IL DIRITTO DI ESSERE BEN NUTRITO. Un mdiús p

Tengo derecho a tener amigos. Tenho o d

나는 이름과 국적을 가질 권리가 있다.

من حقي ان يكون لي منزل I HAVE THE RIGHT NOT TO BE TREATE

J'ai le droit de m'exprimer. Il ull

मुझे सूचित होने का, खुद को हक्क करने का और भाग लेने का अ

אני זכאית לחופש ,לדבר, ולהתבטא בלי חשש מהשלכות.

من حق دارم مورد سوءاستفاده قرار نگیرم.

TENGO DERECHO A N

मुझे देखभाल करने का, बीमारी से बचाव का
और अच्छी तरह से पोषित का अधिकार है

حقي ان يكون لي اصدقاء
Ik heb het recht op een naam

Tenho o direito de falar

J'AI LE DROIT

I HAVE THE RIGHT TO BE LOVED

我有權利擁有一個家庭,

Ik HEB HET RECHT
TE SPELEN